History
Around You

Nick Hunter

Heinemann
LIBRARY

Chicago, Illinois

© 2015 Heinemann Library
an imprint of Capstone Global Library, LLC
Chicago, Illinois

Edited by Catherine Veitch and Gina Kammer
Designed by Steve Mead and Peggie Carley
Picture research by Mica Brancic
Production by Helen McCreath
Originated by Capstone Global Library Ltd
Printed and bound in China by RR Donnelley Asia

18 17 16 15 14
10 9 8 7 6 5 4 3 2 1

Library of Congress Cataloging-in-Publication Data
Cataloging-in-publication information is on file with the Library of Congress.
ISBN 978-1-4846-0230-0 (hardcover)
ISBN 978-1-4846-0234-8 (paperback)
ISBN 978-1-4846-0242-3 (eBook PDF)

Acknowledgments
We would like to thank the following for permission to reproduce photographs: Alamy: John Smith, 24, National Geographic Image Collection, 5, Scottish Viewpoint, 19; Getty Images: cover, Hulton Archive, 6, Hulton Archive/Central Press, 20, Lonely Planet Images/Neil Setchfield, 14, Photolibrary/Spencer Grant, 7, Picture Post/Haywood Magee, 22; iStock: cvoogt, 11, mashabuba, 9; Shutterstock: Antonio Abrignani, 28, Elwood Chu, 4, I. Pilon, 18, Jane Rix, 26, Jorge Salcedo, 10, Kiev.Victor, 15, Tupungato, 13; SuperStock: age fotostock/Richard Levine, 23, age fotostock/Walter Bibikow, 12, The Art Archive, 16, ClassicStock.com, 8, 17, imagebroker.net, 25, Robert Harding Picture Library, 27, Science and Society, 21, UpperCut Images, 29

Every effort has been made to contact copyright holders of material reproduced in this book. Any omissions will be rectified in subsequent printings if notice is given to the publisher.

All the Internet addresses (URLs) given in this book were valid at the time of going to press. However, due to the dynamic nature of the Internet, some addresses may have changed, or sites may have changed or ceased to exist since publication. While the author and publisher regret any inconvenience this may cause readers, no responsibility for any such changes can be accepted by either the author or the publisher.

Contents

Some words are shown in bold, **like this**.
You can find out what they mean by looking
in the glossary.

History and You

When we learn about history, we discover how people lived in the past. We can find out about people who lived hundreds of years ago in faraway parts of the world.

▲ These warrior statues were made more than 2,000 years ago in China.

There is also lots of history in the place where you live. You can find history all around you, in the smallest town or in a busy city. You can find history in your local area in many ways.

Many towns are a mixture of old and modern buildings. Can you spot the old building here?

Changing Times

Look around on your way to school and you will see your neighborhood changing. Look out for new homes being built. You may see a new playground opening or shops closing down.

▲ This is a busy San Francisco street more than 100 years ago.

Over many years, these everyday changes will make your neighborhood very different. The pictures on these pages show how a town has changed over 100 years.

▲ Today the same busy street looks very different.

Asking Questions

If you want to find out about local history, start asking some questions. Your parents and grandparents can tell you how the area has changed since they were at school.

▲ Ask your teachers how your school has changed.

You can use historical sources to find out about local history. **Primary sources** are things that have survived from the time. **Secondary sources** include books or films that were made later.

▲ Old photos are primary sources. They show what people and places looked like in the past.

Homes

Do you live in a new or old home? You may find your house on old photos or maps. If the homes nearby look the same, they were probably all built around the same time.

▲ The buildings in this neighborhood were built more than 100 years ago.

Try to find the oldest homes in your area. Hundreds of years ago, homes were built of wood or stone rather than bricks. Older brick houses were often built for rich people.

▲ Some old wooden houses have been changed or added onto by families that live in them today.

Public Buildings

Many old houses built of wood have been replaced with newer homes. Many public buildings were built of stone so they are still standing. These buildings include town halls or meeting places. You can still visit them today.

▲ This courthouse was built in 1907.

Churches are often the oldest buildings in a town. Local people have been visiting this stone church for hundreds of years. Churches contain records of local people who were members there.

▲ When it was first built, this church would have been taller than the buildings around it.

Remembering People

In churchyards and **cemeteries** you can find the graves of people who lived in the local area. Gravestones show the date people were born and when they died. Richer people built large tombs.

▲ These grand tombs are in Glasgow, Scotland.

Sometimes **monuments** and statues were built to remember people. The names of people who died in a war are often listed on war memorials.

WHO GAVE THEIR LIVES FOR THEIR KING AND COUNTRY DURING THE GREAT WAR 1914-1918 AND OF THE OFFICERS WARRANT OFFICERS NON COMMISSIONED OFFICERS AND MEN OF THE HOUSEHOLD CAVALRY ROYAL REGIMENT OF ARTILLERY CORPS OF ROYAL ENGINEERS ROYAL ARMY SERVICE CORPS ROYAL ARMY MEDICAL CORPS AND OTHER UNITS WHO WHILE SERVING WITH THE GUARDS DIVISION IN FRANCE & BELGIUM 1915-1918 FELL WITH THEM IN THE FIGHT FOR THE WORLD'S FREEDOM

THIS MEMORIAL ALSO COMMEMORATES ALL THOSE MEMBERS OF THE HOUSEHOLD DIVISION WHO DIED IN THE SECOND WORLD WAR AND IN THE SERVICE OF THEIR COUNTRY SINCE 1918

▲ You can find war memorials in many towns and villages.

Pictures and Photographs

Pictures will show you what life was like. Before photographs were invented, artists would paint **portraits** of rich families. Most ordinary people could not afford to pay for portraits.

▲ This picture was painted in 1853. What can it tell us about children's lives at that time?

Old photographs tell us a lot about how people lived. One hundred years ago, photographers took family portraits. The families wore their best clothes. Photos were only in black and white.

▲ Family photos in the past were more serious than photos we take now.

Local Museums

Many places have a local museum. In a big city, a museum can be very large. In a small town, a museum could be in a single room. Museum displays include pictures and objects from the past.

▲ Museums collect ancient objects, such as this stone arrowhead.

The museum may keep old records from your town. Before telephones and the **Internet** were invented, people wrote letters to friends and family. Letters can tell us what people did in their everyday lives.

▲ In the past, important documents were written out by hand and stored in libraries.

Reading the News

Many years ago, newspapers were the only way to find out what was happening in the local area and around the world. Old newspapers will tell you what happened on any day in the past.

▲ These people are buying newspapers to tell them about the first man to travel into space.

Old posters and **advertisements** can also tell us a lot about how people lived in the past. Advertisements were eye-catching or colorful to make people buy things.

This poster is advertising seaside vacations. ▶

CONEY BEACH
PORTHCAWL

WATER-CHUTE

OUTINGS
to Britain's Brightest Pleasure Beach
WRITE MANAGER, CONEY BEACH, PORTHCAWL
FOR ILLUSTRATED BOOKLETS AND MENUS
BRITISH RAILWAYS

Changing Communities

Your town may be home to the children or grandchildren of people who moved from other countries. Your own family may once have lived somewhere very different.

▲ Many **immigrants** moved to the United Kingdom from the Caribbean during the 1950s.

Find out why immigrants from other countries moved to your area. Ask older people what they found difficult when they first arrived. How have things changed since they have lived in your area?

▲ Immigrants often bring colorful festivals and music to their new home countries.

Work and Play

Many jobs that people did in the past are less common today. Factories have closed down. Some factories may have changed into homes or apartments.

▲ This old factory and canal were once used to make and transport goods.

Many sports teams have been part of a local area for many years. When were your local teams started? Your teams may have old photos to help you explore their history.

▲ Compare old photos and modern photos to see how local sports teams have changed.

Famous Events and People

A major historical event could have happened in your area in the past. Look out for special museums or monuments. They may be there to remember a battle or a famous person from your town.

▲ This museum was built to look like the original home of the famous writer William Shakespeare.

Many museums are close to important historic sites. **Archaeologists** dig beneath the ground to find out about people who lived hundreds of years ago.

▲ Many historical clues are hidden under the ground.

Your Local History Project

Find out as much as you can about your local area. Try to find primary sources from your area's past. You can also ask adults for help to **interview** people who have lived in your town for many years.

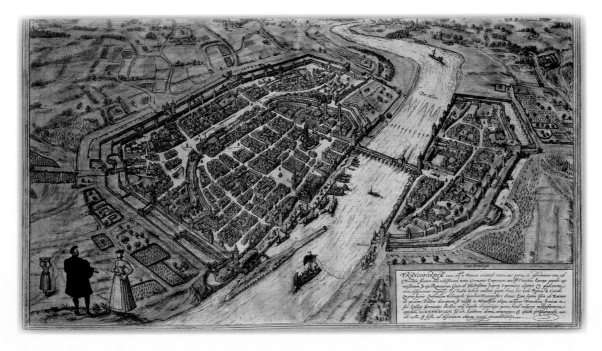

▲ Comparing old and new maps will show how your city has changed. This map was made in 1572.

Collect everything you find out about your area in a scrapbook. If you can collect photos and other information on a computer, it will be easier to share your project with your family and friends.

▲ You could ask your parent or teacher to help you put together a **website** to share what you have learned.

Find Out More

Books

Noon, Steve. *A City Through Time.*
New York: DK Publishing, 2013

Williams, Brian. *Your Local History* (Unlocking History).
Chicago: Raintree, 2010

Websites

http://www.americaslibrary.gov/es/index.php
Learn more about the history of your state.

**www.bbc.co.uk/history/handsonhistory/
local-history.shtml**
See a video guide to researching local history.

**http://memory.loc.gov/ammem/gmdhtml/
cityhome.html**
Find maps of towns and cities and see how they have
changed over the years.

Glossary

advertisement information, such as on a poster or on TV, that tries to make people buy something

archaeologist someone who digs in the ground to uncover remains from the past

cemetery area in many towns and cities where people are buried when they die

immigrant someone who moves to a new country from the country where they were born

Internet system of connected computers that we can use to send and receive information around the world

interview conversation in which one person is being asked lots of questions to get information

monument statue or other object that was put up to remember an event or person

portrait painting or photograph of a person or group of people

primary source object, document, picture, or recording that dates from the time being studied

secondary source source, such as a book, that describes a time but was written or created later

website collection of words, pictures, and other features that can be accessed with a computer via the Internet

Index